Theodore S. Palmer

A list of the generic and family names of rodents

Theodore S. Palmer

A list of the generic and family names of rodents

ISBN/EAN: 9783337716547

Printed in Europe, USA, Canada, Australia, Japan

Cover: Foto ©ninafisch / pixelio.de

More available books at **www.hansebooks.com**

Vol. XI pp. 241-270   December 17, 1897

PROCEEDINGS

OF THE

BIOLOGICAL SOCIETY OF WASHINGTON

A LIST OF THE GENERIC AND FAMILY NAMES OF RODENTS

BY

WASHINGTON, D. C.
PUBLISHED BY THE BIOLOGICAL SOCIETY OF WASHINGTON

VOL. XI, PP. 241-270   DECEMBER 17, 1897

PROCEEDINGS

OF THE

BIOLOGICAL SOCIETY OF WASHINGTON

A LIST OF THE GENERIC AND FAMILY NAMES OF RODENTS.

BY T. S. PALMER.

Generic names of mammals have undergone many changes in recent years, and in no group is this more apparent than in the Rodentia. Not only have new names been proposed for a host of new forms, but many well-known genera now appear under names long forgotten, but revived in obedience to the law of priority. Linnæus, in 1758, recognized only six genera of rodents (including *Rhinoceros!*); Agassiz, in 1842–'46, recorded about 220 generic names in this order, and Marschall, in 1873, added 65 more, making a total of somewhat less than 300. The present list contains more than 600 (a large proportion of which are, of course, synonyms), comprising perhaps 15 percent of the entire number of generic and subgeneric names ever proposed for mammals.

Recent changes in the nomenclature of the Rodentia are well exemplified in two important papers which have appeared during the past few months—one, by Mr. Oldfield Thomas, entitled 'On the Genera of Rodents';[1] the other, by Dr. E. L. Trouessart, comprising part of the second edition of his 'Catalogus Mammalium.' The former paper gives merely a list of the groups of living rodents which the author considers worthy of generic rank, together with references to the original description of each genus. Trouessart's Catalogue, more ambitious in its scope, is

---

[1] Proc. Zool. Soc. London, 1896, pp. 1012–1028.

intended to include all the species, living and extinct, now recognized. Even with these aids the student will often find difficulty in looking up synonymy or determining the earliest name of a genus, for Thomas gives only about one-third of the names, while Trouessart does not pretend to include all the generic synonyms and frequently omits references.

The present paper differs from either of those just mentioned. It is neither an index nor a catalogue of recognized genera, but merely an attempt to bring together *all* the names, generic and subgeneric, ever proposed. It is not complete in itself, inasmuch as it gives neither references to descriptions nor localities; but the authority, date of publication, and type or included species under each name will throw some light on these points. In arranging this list everything has been subordinated to convenience of reference. Genera and subgenera have been treated alike and distributed under families, while the alphabetical arrangement has been followed both in the sequence of higher groups and in the names under each family. Some difficulty has been experienced in properly grouping the genera, and about a dozen names have not been referred to any family for lack of sufficient information regarding their status. Thomas' classification of recent genera has been followed, except in the case of *Lophiomyidæ*, which is given full family rank, instead of being placed as a subfamily under *Muridæ*. To these 22 groups have been added 5 additional families of extinct rodents recognized by Zittel,[1] making a total of 27 families. More than 200 names occur under *Muridæ*, and for simplicity they have been placed under subfamilies, but this is the only instance in which the alphabetical arrangement of the family has not been followed.[2]

The date is always the year of *actual publication*, often very different from the date of apparent publication. For example, the description of *Schizodon* was published in the Proceedings of the Zoological Society of London for 1841, but it did not actually appear until March, 1842. *Arctomys* was described in a part of the fourth volume of Schreber's Säugthiere, issued in 1782, but the name was first published on plates accompanying this work, which are known to have been distributed in 1780. *Schizodon*

---

[1] 'Handbuch der Palæontologie,' IV, 1892–'93.

[2] I am indebted to Mr. Thomas for looking over the genera of *Muridæ* and *Octodontidæ* and for several suggestions as to the arrangement of the list.

is therefore quoted as 1842 and *Arctomys* as 1780.[1] Preoccupied names have been marked, and cross-references made to those proposed to replace them. A few names have become almost unrecognizable by reason of the changes they have undergone in the process of emendation. Among such may be mentioned the correction of *Aplodontia* to *Haploodus, Pithecheir* to *Pithecochirus,* and *Cœlogenus* to *Genyscœlus.*[2] The original spelling is always given, but no attempt has been made to include all variations, although the more important have been noted. If the first letter of a word has been changed, both forms have been inserted in the list, but other changes have been indicated in foot-notes.

Each genus is followed by the type or species on which it was based. When no type was designated and none has been indicated by a subsequent reviser, all the species are mentioned in the order given in the original description. No doubt some errors will be detected here, for at first an attempt was made to determine the types for as many genera as possible. This plan was subsequently abandoned in favor of an enumeration of all the species originally mentioned, but some cases of elimination may have escaped correction.

More or less lack of uniformity exists in the nomenclature of certain families, as, for example, in the cases of the American Porcupines and Chinchillas. Thomas, considering the New World Porcupines worthy of separation, erected the family *Erethizontidæ,* and Trouessart, a few months later, recognized the same group, but renamed it *Coendidæ.* No less than three family designations for the Chinchillas are in common use—*Chinchillidæ, Eriomyidæ,* and *Lagostomyidæ.* Such a condition of things is obviously unnecessary, and can only lead to confusion. As

---

[1] While this paper was in press, my attention was called to Sherborn's announcement of the discovery of Lacépède's well-known 'Tableau Méthodique' (usually quoted 1801), in the Didot edition of Buffon's Histoire Naturelle, Quad., vol. XIV, 1799 (Nat. Sci., XI, p. 432, Dec., 1897). Lacépède's genera *Agouti, Arvicola, Coendou, Hamster, Pika,* and *Talpoides* therefore date from 1799, instead of 1801, but the necessary corrections could only be inserted in the cases of *Pika* and *Talpoides.*

[2] In explanation of this remarkable emendation the author says: " Le *o* grec ne répondant pas à l'u latin, le nom de Cuvier [*Cœlogenus*] n'est pas acceptable, puisqu, il renferme une faute d'orthographie; et, pour faire un nom d'apparence réellement latine, il aurait au moins fallu écrire *Genyscœlus* et non *Cœlogenus.*" Liais, Climats du Bresil, 1872, p. 537.

an aid in selecting the proper name in such cases and to help in determining questions of priority, it has seemed best to give under each group all the family and subfamily names based on genera belonging to it. Full references have also been inserted, inasmuch as authors seldom indicate the place where such names were first published. Groups first described as full families and afterwards reduced to subfamilies have merely a reference to the original description, but those first introduced as subfamilies and afterwards raised to family rank have references to both places of publication. This part of the list has been limited strictly to names ending in ' *idæ* ' or ' *inæ*,' the only exception being old designations with the closely related termination ' *ina.*' Here, as elsewhere, the object has been merely to bring together under each family all the available names, without attempting to discriminate between synonyms and names which have a claim to recognition.[1]

This list is supplementary to a complete alphabetical index of the genera of mammals, containing full references to descriptions and localities, which is now almost ready for the press. The data relating to the Rodentia are here grouped under families and published in condensed form for the purpose of inviting suggestions and criticisms as to arrangement, type species, and grouping of genera. The list is therefore merely an experiment. Although the names have been brought together, much remains to be done in working out the synonymy of types, but such work properly belongs to the specialist and the reviser of groups. When this has been done some examples of duplication of names will probably be found even more striking than the case of the lemmings, in which a single species (*Mus torquatus* Pallas) has served as the basis for five or six nominal genera.

As a help in distinguishing the names, extinct genera are printed in *italics;* an asterisk (*) indicates that the original description has not been seen; a dagger (†) that the name is preoccupied, and a double dagger (‡) prefixed to a family or subfamily that the name is not available, either because the genus on which it was based is preoccupied or because it is antedated by some other valid name.

---

[1] Forsyth Major has recently proposed *Nesomyinæ* for certain Old World mice usually classed under *Cricetinæ*; but as he does not give the limits of this group Thomas' classification is necessarily followed, although *Nesomyinæ* may be entitled to subfamily rank as much as the group under which it is placed.

ANOMALURIDÆ.

Anomalurina GERVAIS, in D'Orbigny's Dict. Univ. d'Hist. Nat., XI, p. 203, 1849.
Anomaluridæ GILL, Arrangement Fam. Mamm., p. 21, Nov., 1872.

Name, authority, and date.	Type or included species.
Anomalurus Waterhouse, 1843.	Anomalurus fraseri.
Aroæthrus Waterhouse, 1843..	Suggested to replace Anomalurus, in case latter is preoccupied.
Idiurus Matschie, 1894........	Idiurus zenkeri.

APLODONTIIDÆ.

Haploodontidæ LILLJEBORG, Syst. Öfversigt Gnag. Däggdjuren, pp. 9, 41, 1866.
Aplodontiidæ THOMAS, Proc. Zool. Soc. London, 1896, p. 1015 (1897).
Aplodontia [1] Richardson, 1829... Aplodontia leporina (=Anisonyx rufa Raf.)

BATHYERGIDÆ.

Bathyergina GERVAIS, in D'Orbigny's Dict. Univ. d'Hist. Nat., XI, p. 203, 1849.
Bathyergidæ BONAPARTE, Conspectus Syst. Mastozoologiæ, 1850.
Georhychinæ GILL, Arrangement Fam. Mamm., p. 20, Nov., 1872.
‡ Orycterideæ LESSON, Nouv. Tableau Règne Animal, Mamm., p. 120, 1842.

Name, authority, and date.	Type or included species.
Bathyergus Illiger, 1811.......	Mus maritimus.
Cœtomys Gray, 1864........	Bathyergus cæcutiens, B. damarensis.
Cryptomys Gray, 1864........	Georychus holosericeus.
* Fossor Forster...............	(?)
Georychus [2] Illiger, 1811	Mus capensis (type), M. talpinus, M. aspalax.
† Heliophobius Peters, 1846.....	Heliophobius argenteo-cinereus.
Heterocephalus Rüppell, 1842.	Heterocephalus glaber.
Myoscalops Thomas, 1890....	New name for Heliophobius Peters.
Orycterus Cuvier, 1829........	Mus maritimus.
Typhloryctes Fitzinger, 1867..	Georychus ochraceo-cinereus, Bathyergus cæcutiens.

[1] Emended to Haplodon (Wagler, 1830), Apludontia, Apludontia, Apluodontia, Haploodon, Haploudon, Hapludon, Haploudontia, Haplodus, Haploodus, Haploudus, and Hapludus. (See Coues, Century Dict., III, p. 2712.)
[2] Emended to Georhychus (Wagner, 1843).

CASTORIDÆ.

Castoridæ GRAY, London Medical Repository, XV, p. 302, April 1, 1821.
Mylagaulidæ COPE, Bull. U. S. Geol. & Geog. Surv. Terr., VI, No. 2, p. 362, Sept. 19, 1881.

Name, authority, and date.	Type or included species.
* *Aulacodon* Kaup, 1832	*Aulacodon typus.*
Castor Linnæus, 1758	Castor fiber (type), C. moschatus.
* *Castoromys* Pomel, 1854	*Chalicomys sigmodus.*
Chalicomys Kaup, 1832	*Chalicomys jaegeri.*
Chelodus Kaup, 1832	*Chelodus typus.*
† *Chloromys*(Meyer)Schlosser, 1884	*Chalicomys eseri.*
Conodontes Laugel, 1862	*Conodontes boisvilletti.*
† *Conodus* Gervais, 1867–'69	Emended form of *Conodontes.*
Diabroticus Pomel, 1848	*Diabroticus schmerlingii.*
Eucastor Leidy, 1858	*Castor tortus.*
Mylagaulus Cope, 1878	*Mylagaulus sesquipedalis.*
Palæocastor Leidy, 1869	*Steneofiber nebrascensis.*
Palaeomys Kaup, 1832	*Palaeomys castoroides.*
Sigmogomphius J. C. Merriam, 1896.	*Sigmogomphius lecontei.*
Steneofiber Geoffroy, 1834	——
Steneotherium Geoffroy, 1833	——
Trogontherium G. Fischer, 1809	*Trogontherium cuvieri, T. werneri.*

CASTOROIDIDÆ.

Castoroididæ J. A. ALLEN, Mon. N. Am. Rodentia, p. 419, Aug., 1877.

Name, authority, and date.	Type or included species.
Amblyrhiza Cope, 1868	*Amblyrhiza inundata.*
Castoroïdes Foster, 1838	*Castoroïdes ohioensis.*
† *Leptomylus* Cope, 1869	Misprint for *Loxomylus.*
Loxomylus Cope, 1869	*Loxomylus longidens.*

CAVIIDÆ.

Caviadæ GRAY, London Medical Repository, XV, p. 304, April 1, 1821.
Hydrocharina GRAY, Thomson's Ann. Philos., XXVI, p. 341, Nov., 1825.
Hydrochoeridæ GILL, Arrangement Fam. Mammals, p. 22, Nov., 1872.
Kerodontina GERVAIS, in D'Orbigny's Dict. Univ. d'Hist. Nat., XI, p. 204, 1849.

Name, authority, and date.	Type or included species.
Anchymis Ameghino, 1886	*Cardiodon leidyi.*
Anoëma F. Cuvier, 1809	Cavia cobaya.
? *Callodontomys* Ameghino, 1889	*Callodontomys vastatus.*
Capiguara Liais, 1872	New name for Hydrochœrus. (Considered preferable by Liais because derived from the Indian name.)

Cardiatherium Ameghino, 1883.. Cardiatherium dœringi.
† Cardiodon Ameghino, 1885...... Cardiodon marshii, C. leidyi. (See Eu-
          cardiodon.)
* Cardiodus Bravard, 1857........ Cardiodus waterhousii, C. medius, C.
          minus, C. dubius.
Cardiomys Ameghino, 1885..... Cardiomys cavinus.
Cavia Pallas, 1766.......... . . Cavia cobaya.
Caviodon Ameghino, 1885...... Caviodon multiplicatus.
† **Ceratodon** Wagler, 1830...... Emended form for Kerodon.
Cerodon Wagler, 1830... ..... Emended form for Kerodon.
Cobaya Cuvier, 1817 .... Cavia cobaya.
Controcaria Burmeister, 1885.... Controcaria matercula.
Diocartherium Ameghino, 1888.. Diocartherium australe.
Dolichotis Desmarest, 1819 ... Cavia patachonica.
Eucardiodon Ameghino, 1891... New name for Cardiodon.
Galea Meyen, 1833............ Galea musteloides.
Hydrochaerus Brisson, 1762... Sus hydrochoeris.
Kerodon F. Cuvier, 1823...... The 'Moco' of Geoffroy.
Mara D'Orbigny, 1829........ Dolichotis patagonica.
Microcavia Gervais & Ameghino, Microcavia typus, M. robusta, M. inter-
  1880.   media, M. dubia.
Neoprocaria Ameghino, 1889.... New name for Procaria Ameghino.
Oromys Leidy, 1853 .... Oromys æsopi.
Orthomyctera Ameghino, 1889... Caria rigens, Orthomyctera vaga, Doli-
          chotis lacunosa, Orthomyctera lata.
Palæocavia Ameghino, 1889..... Caria impar, C. avita, Palæocavia pam-
          paëa, P. minuta.
Phugatherium Ameghino, 1887 .. Phugatherium cataclisticum.
Plexochœrus Ameghino, 1886.... Hydrochœrus paranensis.
Prea Liais, 1872... .. .. New name for Cavia. (Preferred by
          Liais because native name.)
Procardiatherium Ameghino, 1885 Procardiatherium simplicidens.
† Procavia Ameghino, 1885....... Procavia mesopotamica. (See Neopro-
          cavia.)
Scavia Blumenbach, 1802...... Modified form of Cavia.
Strata Ameghino, 1886..... ..... Strata elevata.

CHINCHILLIDÆ.

Chinchillidæ BENNETT, Proc. Zool. Soc. London, 1833, p. 58.
‡ **Eriomyidæ** BURMEISTER, Syst. Uebersicht Thiere Brasil., I, p. 188, 1854.
‡ **Lagostomidæ** "BONAPARTE, Synopsis Vert. Syst., 1837."
Viscachideæ LESSON, Nouv. Tableau Règne Animal, Mamm., p. 104,
  1842.

    Name, authority, and date.   Type or included species.
Briaromys Ameghino, 1889..... Briaromys trouessartianus.
Callomys D'Orbigny & Geoffroy, Callomys viscacia, Mus laniger, Cal-
  1830.   lomys aureus.

Chinchilla Bennett, 1829	Mus laniger.
Colpostemma Ameghino, 1891	*Colpostemma sinuata.*
† *Epiblema* Ameghino, 1886	*Epiblema horridula.* (See *Neoepiblema.*)
Eriomys Lichtenstein, 1829	Eriomys chinchilla.
Euphilus Ameghino, 1889	*Euphilus ambrosettianus, E. kurtzii.*
Gyriabrus Ameghino, 1891	*Gyriabrus glutinatus.*
Lagidium Meyen, 1833	Lagidium peruanum.
Lagostomus Brookes, 1829	Lagostomus trichodactylus.
† **Lagotis** Bennett, 1833	Lagotis cuvieri.
Megamys D'Orb. & Laurillard, 1842.	*Megamys patagonensis.*
Neoepiblema Ameghino, 1889	New name for *Epiblema* Ameghino.
Perimys Ameghino, 1887	*Perimys erutus, P. onustus.*
Pliolagostomus Ameghino, 1887	*Pliolagostomus notatus.*
Potamarchus Burmeister, 1885	*Potamarchus murinus.*
Prolagostomus Ameghino, 1887	*Prolagostomus pusillus, P. dirisus, P. profluens, P. imperialis.*
Scotaeumys Ameghino, 1887	*Scotaeumys imminutus.*
Sphæramys Ameghino, 1887	*Sphæramys irruptus.*
Sphiggomys Ameghino, 1887	*Sphiggomys zonatus.*
Sphodromys Ameghino, 1887	*Sphodromys scalaris.*
Strophostephanos Ameghino, 1891.	*Strophostephanos iheringii.*
Tetrastylus Ameghino, 1886	*Megamys? laevigatus.*
Vizcacia[1] Schinz, 1824 (?)	Vizcacia pamparum.

DASYPROCTIDÆ.

Agoutidæ Gray, London Medical Repository, XV, p. 304, April 1, 1821.

‡ **Chloromina** Gervais, in D'Orbigny's Dict. Univ. d'Hist. Nat., XI, p. 204, 1849.

‡ **Cœlogenina** Gervais, in D'Orbigny's Dict. Univ. d'Hist. Nat., XI, p. 204, 1849.

‡ **Cœlogenyidæ** Burmeister, Syst. Uebers. Thiere Brasil., I, p. 227, 1854.

Dasyporcina Gray, Thomson's Ann. Philos., XXVI, p. 341, Nov., 1825.

Dasyproctina Gray, List Spec. Mamm. Brit. Mus., pp. xxv, 124, 1843.

Dasyproctidæ Bonaparte, Conspectus Syst. Mastozoologiæ, 1850.

Name, authority, and date.	Type or included species.
Agouti Lacépède, 1801	Agouti paca (= Mus paca Linnæus).
Cloromis F. Cuvier, 1812	Includes the agoutis.
Cœlogenus[2] F. Cuvier, 1807	Cœlogenus subniger, C. fulvus.
Cutia Liais, 1872	New name for Dasyprocta Illiger.
Dasyprocta Illiger, 1811	Cavia aguti, C. acuschy.
Genyscœlus Liais, 1872	Emended form for Cœlogenus.
Osteopera Harlan, 1825	Osteopera platycephala.
Paca Fischer, 1814	Paca maculata (= Cavia paca).
Platypyga Illiger, 1811	(?)

---

[1] Viscacia Rafinesque, 1815 (nomen nudum), Rengger, 1830.

[2] Cœlogenus (Griffith, 1827); Caelogenys (Agassiz, 1846); Coelogenys (Illiger, 1811); Genyscœlus (Liais, 1872).

DINOMYIDÆ.

Dinomyidæ Alston, Proc. Zool. Soc. London, 1876, p. 96.
Dinomys Peters, 1873......... Dinomys branickii.

DIPODIDÆ.[1]

Dipodina Bonaparte, "Synopsis Vert. Syst., 1837."
Dipodidæ Waterhouse, Ann. & Mag. Nat. Hist., X, p. 203, Nov., 1842.
Dipodæ Gervais, in D'Orbigny's Dict. Univ. d'Hist. Nat., XI, p. 203, 1849.
Dipsidæ Gray, London Medical Repository, XV, p. 303, April 1, 1821.
‡ Gerboidæ Waterhouse, Charlesworth's Mag. Nat. Hist., III, p. 186, April, 1839.
‡ Ierboidæ Gray, Thomson's Am. Philos., XXVI, p. 341, Nov., 1825.
‡ Jaculina Carus, Handbuch Zool., p. 101, 1868.
‡ Jaculidæ Gill, Arrangement Fam. Mamm., p. 20, Nov., 1872.
Sminthinæ Alston, Proc. Zool. Soc. London, 1876, p. 80.
Sminthidæ Schulze, Schrift. Nat. Ver. Harz., Wernigerode, V, p. 24, 1890.
Zapodidæ Coues, Bull. U. S. Geol. & Geog. Surv. Terr., I, 2d ser., No. 5, p. 253, 1875.

Name, authority, and date.	Type or included species.
Allactaga Cuvier, 1836........	Dipus allactaga.
Beloprymnus Gloger, 1841....	New name for Allactaga.
Cuniculus Brisson, 1762.......	Dipus allactaga.
Dipus Schreber, 1782........ ..	Dipus jaculus, D. sagitta, D. cafer, D. meridianus, D. tamaricinus.
Euchoreutes W. L. Sclater, 1891.	Euchoreutes naso.
† **Halticus** Brandt, 1844.........	Dipus halticus.
Haltomys Brandt, 1844........	Dipus aegyptius, D. hirtipes, D. macrotarsus, D. mauritanicus.
Jaculus Erxleben, 1777........	Jaculus orientalis, J. giganteus, J. torridarum.
† **Meriones** Cuvier, 1825	Dipus americanus.
Platycercomys Brandt, 1844..	Dipus platyurus.
Pygeretmus Gloger, 1841......	Dipus platyurus.
Scarturus Gloger, 1841........	4-toed species of Dipus.
Scirteta Brandt, 1844...	(?)
Scirtetes Wagner, 1841........	New name for Allactaga Cuvier.
Scirtomys Brandt, 1844.......	Alactaga tetradactylus (= Scarturus Gloger, 1841).
Scirtopoda Brandt, 1844......	Dipus halticus, D. aegyptius, D. hirtipes, D. macrotarsus, D. mauritanicus (= Halticus + Haltomys).

[1] Sminthus represents the subfamily Sminthinæ, Zapus the Zapodinæ, and the other genera belong to the Dipodinæ.

Sminthus Keys. & Blasius,1840.   Sminthus nordmanni.
Yerbua Forster, 1778..........   Yerbua tarsata (- - Tarsius spectrum),
                                     Y. sibirica, Y. capensis (= Pedetes
                                     cafer), Mus meridianus, Yerbua
                                     kanguru (= Macropus giganteus);
                                     Mus longipes, M. jaculus, M. sagitta.
Zapus Coues, 1875.............   Dipus hudsonius.

EOCARDIDÆ.

Eocardidæ Ameghino, Revista Argentina, I, Ent. 3, p. 145, Junio, 1891.

Name, authority, and date.	Type or included species.
Dicardia Ameghino, 1891......	*Dicardia maxima, D. modica, D. excavata.*
Eocardia Ameghino, 1887.......	*Eocardia montana.*
Hedymys Ameghino, 1887.......	*Hedymys integrus.*
Phanomys Ameghino, 1887......	*Phanomys mixtus.*
Procardia Ameghino, 1891	*Eocardia eliptica.*
Schistomys Ameghino, 1887......	*Schistomys erro.*
Tricardia Ameghino, 1891......	*Eocardia divisa.*

ERETHIZONTIDÆ.

‡ **Cercolabina** GRAY, List Spec. Mamm. Brit. Mus., pp. xxiv, 123, 1843.
‡ **Cercolabinæ** GILL, Arrangement Fam. Mamm., p. 22, Nov., 1872.
‡ **Cercolabidæ** AMEGHINO, Enum. Sist. Mam. Fós. Patagonia Austral,
    p. 9, Dic. 1887.
Chætomyinæ THOMAS, Proc. Zool. Soc. London, 1896, 1026 (1897).
Coendidæ TROUESSART, Cat. Mamm. tam viv. quam foss., fasc. III,
    p. 619, Oct., 1897.
Erethizontina BONAPARTE, Conspectus Syst. Mastozoologiæ, 1850.
Erethizontidæ THOMAS, Proc. Zool. Soc. London, 1896, 1025 (Apr., 1897).
‡ **Sphingurinæ** ALSTON, Proc. Zool. Soc. London, 1876, p. 93.
‡ **Synetherina** GERVAIS, in D'Orbigny's Dict. Univ. d'Hist. Nat., XI,
    p. 204, 1849.
‡ **Synetherinæ** TROUESSART, Cat. Mamm. Viv. et Foss., Rongeurs, p. 182,
    1881.

Name, authority, and date.	Type or included species.
Acaremys Ameghino, 1887......	*Acaremys murinus, A. minutus, A. minutissimus.*
Cercolabes Brandt, 1835......	New name for Coendou Lacépède,1801.
Chætomys Gray, 1843........	Hystrix subspinosus.
Coendou[1] Lacépède, 1801......	Hystrix prehensilis.
Echinoprocta Gray, 1865......	Erethizon rufescens.
Echinothrix Brookes, 1828. ..	Hystrix dorsata.

---

[1] Emended to Coendous (Temminck, 1820); Coëndus (Illiger, 1815);
Cœndus (Rafinesque, 1815); Cuandu (Liais, 1872).

Erethizon[1] F. Cuvier, 1822..... Hystrix dorsata.
Hystricops Leidy, 1858.......... *Hystrix venustus.*
Onychura Brookes, 1828....... Onychura spinosa.
Plectrochœrus Pictet, 1843.... Plectrochœrus moricandi.
Sciamys Ameghino, 1887........ *Sciamys principalis, S. varians.*
Siuœtherus[2] F. Cuvier, 1822... Hystrix prehensilis.
Sphiggurus[3] F. Cuvier, 1822... Sphiggurus spinosus,
Steiromys Ameghino, 1887....... *Steiromys detentus, S. duplicatus.*

GEOMYIDAE.

Geomyina Bonaparte, Conspectus Syst. Mastozoologiæ, 1850.
Geomyinæ Baird, Mamm. N. Am., pp. xxx, 366, 1857.
Geomyidæ Gill, Arrangement Fam. Mamm., p. 21, Nov., 1872.
‡ Pseudotomina Gray, Thomson's Ann. Philos., XXVI, p. 342, 1825.
‡ Pseudostomidæ Gervais, Ann. Sci. Nat., Paris, 3e ser., XX, p. 245, 1853.

Name, authority, and date.	Type or included species.
Ascomys Lichtenstein, 1825...	Ascomys canadensis (= Mus bursarius).
Cratogeomys Merriam, 1895...	Geomys merriami.
Diplostoma Rafinesque, 1817..	Diplostoma fusca (= Mus bursarius).
Geomys Rafinesque, 1817......	Geomys pinetis (= Mus tuza Ord).
Gymnoptychus Cope, 1873.......	*Gymnoptychus chrysodon, G. nasutus,* G. trilophus, and G. minutus.
Heliscomys Cope, 1873..........	*Heliscomys vetus.*
Heterogeomys Merriam, 1895.	Geomys hispidus.
Macrogeomys Merriam, 1895..	Geomys heterodus.
Orthogeomys Merriam, 1895...	Geomys scalops.
Oryctomys Eydoux & Gervais, 1836.	Five subgenera: Diplostoma, Saccophorus, Saccomys, Poephagomys, Ctenomys.
Pappogeomys Merriam, 1895..	Geomys bulleri.
Platygeomys Merriam, 1895...	Geomys gymnurus.
Pseudostoma Say, 1823.......	Pseudostoma bursaria.
Saccophorus Kuhl, 1820.......	Mus bursarius.
Thomomys Maximilian, 1839..	Thomomys rufescens.
*?Tucanus Rafinesque, 1815.....	Nomen nudum?
Zygogeomys Merriam, 1895...	Zygogeomys trichopus.

---

[1] Emended to Erethison (Waterhouse, 1839); Eretison (McMurtrie, 1831); Eretizon (Cuvier, 1825); Erythizon (Alston, 1876).

[2] Emended to Sinetheres (Agassiz, 1842); Sinœtherus (Cuvier, 1825); Synætheres (Gervais, 1859); Synetheres (G. Cuvier, 1829); Synœtheres (Lund, 1839).

[3] Emended to Sphingurus (Waterhouse, 1848); Spiggurus (Gray, 1847); Spigurus (Swainson, 1835).

GLIRIDÆ.[1]

Gliridæ Thomas, Proc. Zool. Soc. London, 1896, 1016 (1897).
‡ **Myosidæ** Gray, London Medical Repository, XV, p. 303, April 1, 1821·
‡ **Myoxidæ** Waterhouse, Charlesworth's Mag. Nat. Hist., III, p. 184,
    April, 1839.
Platacanthomyinæ Alston, Proc. Zool. Soc. London, 1876, p. 81.

Name, authority, and date.	Type or included species.
Bifa Lataste, 1885.	Bifa lerotina.
Brachymys Meyer, 1847.	New name for *Micromys* Meyer, 1846.
Cænomys (Bravard MS.) Lydekker, 1885.	*Cænomys typus* (= *Myoxus murinus*).
Claviglis Jentink, 1888.	Claviglis crassicaudatus.
Eliomys Wagner, 1843.	Myoxus melanurus.
Glis Brisson, 1762.	Sciurus glis.
Graphiurus F. Cuvier, 1838.	Graphiurus capensis.
*†Micromys Meyer, 1846.	*Micromys ornatus.* (See *Brachymys*.)
Muscardinus Kaup, 1829.	Myoxus muscardinus.
Myoxus Schreber, 1782.	Myoxus glis, M. dryas, M. nitela, M. muscardinus.
Platacanthomys Blyth, 1859.	Platacanthomys lasiurus.
Typhlomys Milne Edwards, 1877.	Typhlomys cinereus.

HETEROMYIDÆ.

Dipodomyna Gervais, Ann. Sci. Nat., Paris, 3ᵉᵐᵉ ser., XX, p. 245, 1853.
Dipodomyinæ Coues, Proc. Acad. Nat. Sci. Phila., 1875, p. 277.
Heteromyina Gray, Proc. Zool. Soc. London, 1868, p. 201.
Heteromyinæ Alston, Proc. Zool. Soc. London, 1876, p. 88.
Heteromyidæ Allen, Bull. Am. Mus. Nat. Hist. N.Y., V, p. 233, Sept.
    21, 1893.
Perognathidinæ Coues, Proc. Acad. Nat. Sci. Phila., 1875, pp. 277–278.
‡ **Saccomyna** Gray, List. Spec. Mamm. Brit. Mus., pp. xxiv, 120, 1843.
‡ **Saccomyidæ** Baird, Mamm. N. Am., pp. xxx, 365, 1857.

Name, authority, and date.	Type or included species.
Abromys Gray, 1868	Abromys lordi.
Chætodipus Merriam, 1889	Perognathus spinatus.
Cricetodipus Peale, 1848	Cricetodipus parvus.
Dasynotus Wagler, 1830	Mus anomalus.
Dipodomys Gray, 1841	Dipodomys phillipii
Dipodops Merriam, 1890	Dipodomys agilis.
? *Entoptychus* Cope, 1878	*Entoptychus carifrons, E. planifrons, E. crassiramis.*
Heteromys Desmarest, 1817	Mus anomalus.
Macrocolus Wagner, 1844	Macrocolus halticus.

---

[1] Platacanthomys and Typhlomys belong to the Platacanthomyinæ, the others to the Glirinæ.

Microdipodops Merriam, 1891. Microdipodops megacephalus.
Otognosis Coues, 1875......... Otognosis longimembris.
Perodipus Fitzinger, 1867..... Dipodomys agilis.
Perognathus Maximilian, 1839. Perognathus fasciatus.
Pleurolicus Cope, 1878......... *Pleurolicus sulcifrons.*
Saccomys F. Cuvier, 1823..... Saccomys anthophilus.

HYSTRICIDAE.

Histricidæ GRAY, London Med. Repository, XV, p. 304, April 1, 1821.
Hystrixideæ LESSON, Nouv. Tableau Règne Animal, Mamm., p. 96, 1842.

Name, authority, and date.	Type or included species.
Acantherium Gray, 1847......	Acanthion javanicum, A. flemingii.
Acanthion Cuvier, 1822.......	Acanthion javanicum.
Acanthochoerus Gray, 1866...	Acanthochoerus bartlettii, A. grotei.
Atherurus F. Cuvier, 1829.....	Hystrix fasciculata.
* **Eucritus** G. Fischer, 1817.....	(?)
Hystricotherium Croizet, 1853 ...	*Hystrix refossa.*
Hystrix Linnæus, 1758........	Hystrix cristata, H. prehensilis, H. dorsata, H. macroura, H. brachyura.
Lamprodon Wagner, 1848.......	*Lamprodon primigenius.*
Œdocephalus Gray, 1866......	Acanthion cuvieri.
* *Oreomys* Aymard, 1854........	*Oreomys claveris.*
Trichys Günther, 1876........	Trichys lipura.

ISCHYROMYIDÆ.

Ischyromyidæ ALSTON, Proc. Zool. Soc. London, 1876, pp. 67, 78.

Name, authority, and date.	Type or included species.
Colonomys Marsh, 1872.........	*Colonomys celer.*
Colotaxis Cope, 1873...........	*Colotaxis cristatus.*
Ischyromys Leidy, 1856.........	*Ischyromys typus.*
? *Mysops* Leidy, 1871............	*Mysops minimus.*
Paramys Leidy, Nov. 28, 1871..	*Paramys delicatus, P. delicatior, P. delicatissimus.*
Pseudotomus Cope, 1872........	*Pseudotomus hians.*
Sciuravus Marsh, June 21, 1871.	*Sciuravus nitidus, S. undans.*
? *Sciuromys* Schlosser, 1884	*Sciuromys cayluxi.*
Syllophodus Cope, 1881........	New name for *Mysops* Leidy, 1871 (erroneously said to be preoccupied).
Taxymys Marsh, 1872..........	*Taxymys lucaris.*
Tillomys Marsh, 1872..........	*Tillomys senex, T. parvus.*

LEPORIDÆ.

Lagidæ SCHULZE, Helios, XIV, p. 82, 1897.
Leporidæ GRAY, London Medical Repository, XV, p. 304, April 1, 1821.
Lepusidæ GERVAIS, Ann. Sci. Nat., 3ᵐᵉ ser., XX, p. 246, 1853.

Name, authority, and date.	Type or included species.
Caprolagus Blyth, 1845........	Lepus hispidus.
Chionobates Kaup, 1829......	Lepus variabilis, L. borealis.
† **Cuniculus** Gloger, 1841.......	Lepus cuniculus.
Eulagos Gray, 1867...........	Lepus mediterraneus, L. judææ.
† **Hydrolagus** Gray, 1867	Lepus aquaticus (type), L. palustris. (See Limnolagus).
Lagopsis Rafinesque, 1815.....	Nomen nudum.
* **Lagos** Brookes, 1828..........	Lepus arcticus.
Lagotherium Croizet, 1853......	*Lepus issiodorensis, L. neschersensis.*
Lepus Linnæus, 1758.........	Lepus timidus, L. cuniculus, L. capensis, L. brasiliensis.
Limnolagus Mearns, 1897.....	New name for Hydrolagus Gray, 1867.
Macrotolagus Mearns, 1895...	Lepus alleni.
Microlagus Trouessart, 1897...	Lepus cinerascens.
Oryctolagus Lilljeborg, 1873...	Lepus cuniculus.
Palæolagus Leidy, 1856........	*Palæolagus haydeni.*
Panolax Cope, 1874..........	*Panolax sanctæfidei.*
Praotherium Cope, 1871........	*Praotherium palatinum.*
Romerolagus Merriam, 1896...	Romerolagus nelsoni.
Sylvilagus Gray, 1867.	Lepus nanus (= L. americanus), L. artemisia (= L. nuttalli), L. bachmani.
Tapeti Gray, 1867............	Lepus brasiliensis.
Tricium Cope, 1873............	*Tricium arunculus, T. leporinum, T. paniense.*

LOPHIOMYIDÆ.

Lophiomyidæ GILL, Arrangement Fam. Mamm., p. 20, Nov., 1872.
   Lophiomys Milne Edwards, Feb. 6, 1867. Lophiomys imhausii.
   Phractomys Peters, Feb., 1867.......... Phractomys aethiopicus.

MURIDÆ.

CRICETINÆ.

Cricetina GRAY, Thomson's Ann. Philos., XXVI, p. 342, Nov., 1825.
Cricetinæ ALSTON, Proc. Zool. Soc. London, 1876, p. 82.
Cricetidæ ZITTEL, Handbuch d. Palæontologie, IV, 2ᵗᵉ Lief., p. 534, 1893.
Hesperomyidæ AMEGHINO, Mam. Fós., in Actas Acad. Nac. Ciencias, Córdoba, VI, p. 109, 1889.
Nesomyinæ FORSYTH MAJOR, Proc. Zool. Soc. London, 1897, p. 718.
Sigmodontinæ THOMAS, Proc. Zool. Soc. London, 1896, 1019 (1897).

Name, authority, and date.	Type or included species.
Abrothrix Waterhouse, 1837...	Mus (Abrothrix) longipilis.
Acromys ('Wagner') Trouessart, 1881. Synonym of Drymomys.
Akodon Meyen, 1833.........	Akodon boliviense.
Baiomys True, 1894..........	Hesperomys taylori.

Blarinomys Thomas, 1896..... Oxymycterus breviceps.
Brachytarsomys Günther, 1875 Brachytarsomys albicauda.
Brachyuromys Forsyth Major, 1896. Brachyuromys ramirohitra.
† **Calomys** Waterhouse, 1837.... Mus (Calomys) bisulcatus.
Chilomys Thomas, 1897....... Oryzomys instans.
Cricetodon Lartet, 1851......... *Cricetodon sansaniensis, C. medium, C. minus.*
Cricetulus Edwards, 1867..... Cricetulus griseus.
Cricetus Zimmermann, 1777... Le Hamster.
Decticus Aymard, 1853...... ... *Decticus antiquus.*
Deilemys Saussure, 1860....... Hesperomys toltecus.
Drymomys Tschudi, 1844.... . Drymomys parvulus.
Eligmodontia[1] F. Cuvier, 1837. Eligmodontia typus.
Eliurus Edwards 1885......... Eliurus myoxinus.
? *Eomys* Schlosser, 1884 .... *Eomys zitteli.*
Eumys Leidy, 1856............ *Eumys elegans.*
Euneomys Coues, 1874........ Reithrodon chinchilloides.
Gymnuromys Forsyth Major, 1896 Gymnuromys roberti.
Habrothrix Wagner, 1843..... Emended form for Abrothrix.
Hallomys Jentink, 1879....... Hallomys audeberti.
Hamster Lacépède, 1801....... Hamster nigricans.
Heligmodontia Agassiz, 1846.. Emended form for Eligmodontia.
Hesperomys Waterhouse, 1839. Mus bimaculatus.
Holochilomys ('Brandt') Pe- Mus aquaticus, M. squamipes (modi-
ters, 1861. fied form of Holochilus).
Holochilus Brandt, 1835 ..... Mus (Holochilus) leucogaster, M. an-
guya.
Hypogeomys Grandidier, 1869. Hypogeomys antimena.
Ichthyomys Thomas, 1893.... Ichthyomys stolzmanni.
* *Lithomys* Meyer, 1846.......... *Lithomys parvulus.*
Megalomys Trouessart, 1881... Mus pilorides.
*† *Micromys* Aymard, 1848........ *Micromys minutus.* (See *Myotherium.*)
* *Myarion* Pomel, 1854........... *Myarion antiquum, M. musculoides, M. minutum, M. angustidens.*
Myotherium Aymard, 1853 ..... New name for *Micromys* Aymard, 1848.
Myoxomys Tomes, 1861....... Hesperomys (Myoxomys) salvinii.
Mystromys Wagner, 1841..... Mystromys albipes.
Necromys Ameghino, 1889 ..... *Necromys conifer.*
Nectomys Peters, 1861........ Mus squamipes, Nectomys apicalis.
† **Neomys** Gray, 1873............ Neomys panamensis.
Neotomys Thomas, 1894...... Neotomys ebriosus.
Nesomys Peters, 1870........ Nesomys rufus.
Notiomys Thomas, 1890....... Hesperomys (Notiomys) edwardsii.
Nyctomys Saussure, 1860...... Hesperomys sumichrasti.
Ochetodon Coues, 1874........ Mus humilis.

---

[1] Emended to *Eligmodon* (Thomas, 1896), *Elimodon* (Fitzinger, 1867), and *Heligmodontia* (Agassiz, 1846).

Onychomys Baird, 1857.......	Hypudæus leucogaster.
* **?Orycteromys** Pictet, 1842......	(?)
Oryzomys Baird, 1857.........	Mus palustris.
Oxymycterus Waterhouse, 1837	Mus (Oxymycterus) nasutus.
* **Pelamys** Jourdan, 1867 (?).....	Pelamys remifer.
Peromyscus Gloger, 1841..	Peromyscus arboreus (= Cricetus my-oides).
Phyllotis Waterhouse, 1837....	Mus (Phyllotis) darwini.
Reithrodon [1] Waterhouse, 1837.	Reithrodon typicus, R. cuniculoïdes.
Reithrodontomys Giglioli, 1873	Reithrodon from North America.
Rhipidomys Tschudi, 1844....	Hesperomys leucodactylus.
Scapteromys Waterhouse, 1837	Mus (Scapteromys) tumidus.
Sigmodon Say & Ord, 1825....	Sigmodon hispidum.
Sigmodontomys J. A. Allen, 1897.	Sigmodontomys alfari.
Sitomys Fitzinger, 1867.......	Cricetus myoides.
Thomasomys Coues, 1884.....	Hesperomys cinereus.
Trinodontomys Rhoads, 1894.	Sitomys insolatus.
Tylomys Peters, 1866.....	Hesperomys (Tylomys) nudicaudus.
Vesperimus Coues, 1874.......	Hesperomys (Vesperimus) leucopus.
Vesperomys ('Coues') Alston, 1880.	Modified form of Vesperimus.
Zygodontomys J. A. Allen, 1897	Oryzomys cherriei.

DENDROMYINÆ.

Dendromyinæ ALSTON, Proc. Zool. Soc. London, 1876, p. 82.
Deomyinæ LYDEKKER, in Flower & Lydekker's Mamm., Living & Extinct, p. 473, 1891.

Name, authority, and date.	Type or included species.
Dendromus A. Smith, 1829....	Dendromus typus.
Deomys Thomas, 1888........	Deomys ferrugineus.
Leimacomys [2] Matschie, 1893..	Leimacomys büttneri.
Malacothrix Wagner, 1843....	New name for Otomys Smith, 1834.
† **Otomys** Smith, 1834..........	Otomys typicus, O. albicaudatus.
Steatomys Peters, 1846........	Steatomys pratensis.

GERBILLINÆ.

Gerbillina GRAY, Thomson's Ann. Philos., XXVI, p. 342, Nov., 1825.
Gerbillidæ DE KAY, Nat. Hist. New York, Zool., pt. I, pp. xv, 70, 1842.

Name, authority, and date.	Type or included species.
Amphiaulacomys Lataste, 1882.	Rhombomys pallidus.
Dipodillus Lataste, 1881.......	Gerbillus simoni.
Endecapleura Lataste, 1882...	Gerbillus garamantis.
Gerbillus Desmarest, 1804.....	Gerbillus ægyptius, G. canadensis, G. pyramidum.
Hendecapleura Thomas, 1883..	Emended form for Endecapleura.

[1] Emended to Rhithrodon (Lydekker, 1891), Rithrodon (Agassiz, 1846).
[2] Emended to Limacomys (Lydekker, 1894).

Meriones Illiger, 1811..... ... Dipus tamaricinus, D. meridianus.
Pachyuromys Lataste, 1880... Pachyuromys duprasi.
Psammomys Cretzschmar, 1828. Psammomys obesus.
Rhombomys Wagner, 1841.... Rhombomys pallidus.
Tatera Lataste, 1882.......... Gerbillus indicus.

HYDROMYINÆ·

Hydromyina Gray, Thomson's Ann. Philos., XXVI, p. 341, Nov., 1825.
Hydromyinæ Alston, Proc. Zool. Soc. London, 1876, p. 80.
Hydromysideæ Lesson, Nouv. Tabl. Règne Animal, Mamm., p. 125, 1842.

Name, authority, and date.	Type or included species.
Chrotomys Thomas, 1895. ...	Chrotomys whiteheadi.
Hydromys Geoffroy, 1805......	Mus coypus, Hydromys chrysogaster, H. leucogaster.
Xeromys Thomas, 1889......	Xeromys myoides.

MICROTINÆ.

‡ **Arvicolidæ** Gray, London Med. Repository, XV, p. 303, April 1, 1821.
‡ **Ellobiinae** [1] Gill, Arrangement Fam. Mamm., p. 20, Nov., 1872.
Lemnina Gray, Thomson's Ann. Philos., XXVI, p. 342, Nov., 1825.
Microtinæ Rhoads, Am. Nat., XXIX, p. 940, Oct., 1895.
    Miller, N. Am. Fauna, No. 12, p. 8, July, 1896.
‡ **Ondatrina** Gray, Thomson's Ann. Philos., XXVI, p. 341, Nov., 1825.

Name, authority, and date.	Type or included species.
Agricola Blasius, 1857.........	Arvicola agrestis.
Alticola Blanford, 1881........	Arvicola stoliczkanus.
Alviceola Blainville, 1817......	'Le genre campagnol.' (Misprint for Arvicola?)
Ammomys Bonaparte, 1831...	New name for Psammomys Le Conte.
Anaptogonia Cope, 1871........	*Arvicola hiatidens.*
Anteliomys Miller, 1896......	Microtus chinensis.
Arvicola Lacépède, 1801.......	Mus amphibius (= M. terrestris Linn.)
Aulacomys Rhoads, 1894	Aulacomys arvicoloides.
Bicunedens Hodgson, 1863....	Bicunedens perfuscus (nomen nudum = Neodon sikimensis).
Borioikon Poliakoff, 1881.....	Myodes torquatus.
Brachyurus Fischer, 1813.....	Mus arvalis, M. rutilus, M. amphibius, M. lemmus, M. torquatus, M. alliarius, Brachyurus blumenbachii, B. fulvus, B. niloticus.
Bramus Pomel, 1892......	*Bramus barbarus.*
† **Campicola** Schulze, 1890	Arvicola arvalis, A. subterraneus, A. campestris.
Chilotus Baird, 1857.....	Arvicola oregoni.

---

[1] Preoccupied by Ellobiinæ, a subfamily of Mollusks. See Adams, Gen. Recent Moll., II, p. 237, 1858.

* **Chthonoergus** Nordmann, 1839. Mus murinus (= M. talpinus Pallas).
† **Cuniculus** Wagler, 1830....... Mus lemmus, M. torquatus (type), M. aspalax. (See Borioikon, Dicrostonyx, Misothermus, Tylonyx.)
Dicrostonyx Gloger, 1841..... Mus hudsonius?
† **Ellobius** Fischer, 1814......... Mus talpinus (type), Ellobius zocor (= Mus aspalax), Mus capensis, M. hudsonius.
Eothenomys Miller, 1896...... Microtus melanogaster.
Eremiomys Poliakoff, 1881 ... Georychus luteus, Mus lagurus (type).
Evotomys Coues, 1874........ Mus rutilus.
Fiber Cuvier, 1800............ Castor zibethicus.
*†**Glareolus** Oken, 1816......... Mus arvalis, M. campestris?
H e m i o t o m y s Sélys-Long- Arvicola fulvus (= A. arvalis), A. am-
champs, 1836.   phibius (= A. terrestris).
Hyperacrius Miller, 1896...... Microtus fertilis.
Hypudaeus Illiger, 1811....... Mus lemmus, M. amphibius (= M. terrestris), M. arvalis.
Isodelta Cope, 1871...... ..... *Arvicola speothen.*
Lagurus Gloger, 1841.......... Lagurus migratorius (= Mus lagurus Pall. ?)
Lasiopodomys Lataste, 1887.. Arvicola brandti.
Lemmomys Lesson, 1842 ..... Mus talpinus.
* **Lemmus** Link, 1795........... Mus socialis, M. lagurus, M. lemmus (type), M. torquatus, M. glareolus, M. hudsonius.
Microtus Schrank, 1798....... Mus terrestris (= M. arvalis Pall., type), M. amphibius (= M. terrestris Linn.), M. gregarius (= M. arvalis Pall. ?)
† **Micrurus** Forsyth Major, 1876. Arvicola nebrodensis.
Mictomys True, 1894......... Mictomys innuitus.
Misothermus Hensel, 1855..... Myodes torquatus.
Mussascus Oken, 1816........ Ondatra americana (= Castor zibethicus).
Mynomes[1] Rafinesque, 1817... Mynomes pratensis (= Arvicola pennsylvanicus).
[**Myocastor** Kerr, 1792........ Mus Myocaster coypus (type), Mus M. zibethicus. (See Octodontidæ.)]
Myodes Pallas, 1811........... Mus lemmus, M. torquatus, M. lagurus, M. oeconomus, M. arvalis, M. saxatilis, M. gregalis, M. socialis, M. alliarius, M. rutilus.
* *Myolemmus* Pomel, 1854........ *Myolemmus ambiguus.*
Neodon Hodgson, 1849........ Neodon sikimensis.
Neofiber True, 1884........... Neofiber alleni.

---

[1] Emended to Myonomes (Coues, 1874).

Ochetomys Fitzinger, 1867....	Mus amphibius, Hypudæus pertinax, Arvicola destructor, Mus terrestris, Hypudæus nageri, Arvicola monticola, A. americanus.	
* **Oudatra** Link, 1795..........	Ondatra coypus, O. zibethicus.	
† **Paludicola** Blasius, 1857.......	Arvicola amphibius (= A. terrestris), A. nivalis, A. ratticeps.	
Pedomys Baird, 1857.........	Arvicola austerus.	
* **Phaiomys** Blyth, 1863.	Phaiomys leucurus (= Microtus blythi Blan.)	
Phenacomys Merriam, 1889...	Phenacomys intermedius.	
Pinemys Lesson, 1836....	Psammomys pinetorum.	
Pitymys McMurtrie, 1831.....	New name for Psammomys Le Conte.	
† **Praticola** Fatio, 1867.........	Arvicola amphibius (= A. terrestris), A. nivalis, A. arvalis, A. ratticeps, A. campestris.	
† **Psammomys** Le Conte, 1830....	Psammomys pinetorum. (See Ammomys, Pinemys, Pitymys.)	
* **Simotes** Fischer, 1829 (?).. ...	(?)	
† **Sylvicola** Fatio, 1867..... ...	Arvicola agrestis.	
Synaptomys Baird, 1857......	Synaptomys cooperi.	
† **Terricola** Fatio, 1867	Arvicola subterraneus, A. savii.	
Tetramerodon Rhoads, 1894...	Arvicola tetramerus.	
Tylonyx Schulze, 1897........	Mus torquatus.	

MURINÆ.

Muridæ Gray, London Medical Repository, XV, p. 303, April 1, 1821.
Musideæ Lesson, Nouv. Tableau Règne Animal, Mamm., p. 134, 1842.

Name, authority, and date.	Type or included species.
Acanthomys Lesson, 1842....	Mus setifer, M. alexandrinus, Acanthomys perchal, Mus platythrix, M. hispidus.
† **Acanthomys** Gray, 1867......	Acanthomys leucopus.
Acomys Geoffroy, 1838........	Mus cahirinus.
Acosminthus Gloger, 1841....	Mus cahirinus, M. dimidiatus.
Apodemus Kaup, 1829........	Mus agrarius.
Arvicanthis Lesson, 1842......	Lemmus niloticus.
Bandicota Gray, 1873........	Bandicota gigantea.
Batomys Thomas, 1895........	Batomys grantii.
Carpomys Thomas, 1895.	Carpomys melanurus.
Chiropodomys Peters, 1868...	Chiropodomys penicillatus.
Chiruromys Thomas, 1888.....	Chiruromys forbesi.
Conilurus Ogilby, 1838........	Conilurus destructor.
Crateromys Thomas, 1895.....	Phlœomys schadenbergi.
Craurothrix Thomas, 1895.....	New name for Echiothrix Gray, 1867.
Cricetomys Waterhouse, 1840.	Cricetomys gambianus.
Dasymys Peters, 1875........	Dasymys gueinzii.

† **Echiothrix**[1] Gray, 1867........ Echiotlirix leucura. (See Craurothrix.)
? *Elomys* Aymard, 1848.... ..... *Elomys priscus.*
Epimys Trouessart, 1881....... 'Gymnomys et Acanthomys p. Gray, 1867 ' (57 species, including Mus caraco, decumanus, rattus, etc.).
Euchætomys Fitzinger, 1867.. Mus palmarum, M. novarae, M. setifer, M. perchal, M. kok, M. hardwickii, M. rufescens, M. ellioti, M. lepidus, M. vittatus, M. pumilio, M. parduleus, M. zebra, Rattus donovani.
Golunda Gray, 1837.......... Golunda ellioti, G. meltada, Mus barbara.
Gymnomys Gray, 1867........ Mus (Gymnomys) celebensis.
Hapalomys Blyth, 1859....... Hapalomys longicaudatus.
† **Hapalotis** Lichtenstein, 1829... Hapalotis albipes.
Heliomys Gray, 1873......... Heliomys jeudei.
Isomys Sundevall, 1842....... Mus variegatus (=Lemmus niloticus).
† **Lasiomys** Peters, 1866. .... Lasiomys afer. (See Lophuromys.)
Leggada Gray, 1837.......... Leggada booduga, Mus platythrix.
Lemniscomys Trouessart, 1881. Mus barbarus, pulchellus, zebra, lineatus, lineato-affinis, pumilio, trivirgatus, dorsalis, univittatus.
† *Lophiomys* Depéret, 1890........ *Lophiomys pyrenaicus.* (See *Trilophomys*).
Lophuromys Peters, 1874...... New name for Lasiomys Peters, 1866.
Malacomys Edwards, 1877.... Malacomys longipes.
Mastacomys Thomas, 1882.... Mastacomys fuscus.
Micromys Dehne, 1841..... .. Micromys agilis.
Murinus Rafinesque, 1815... . Nomen nudum.
Mus Linnæus, 1758.......... Mus porcellus, M. leporinus, M. lemmus, M. marmota, M. monax, M. cricetus, M. terrestris, M. amphibius, M. rattus, M. musculus, M. avellanarius, M. sylvaticus, M. striatus, M. longipes, M. jaculus, M. volans.
Musculus Rafinesque, 1814 ... Musculus frugivorus, M. dichrurus. (Modified form, proposed to supercede Mus).
Nannomys Peters, 1876....... Mus (Nannomys) setulosus.
Nesokia Gray, 1842.......... Mus hardwickii.
Notomys Lesson, 1842........ Dipus mitchellii.
Pelomys Peters, 1852..... ... Mus (Pelomys) fallax.
Pithecheir[2] Cuvier, 1838...... Pithecheir melanurus.
Pogonomys Edwards, 1877.... Mus (Pogonomys) macrourus.

---

[1] Echinothrix Alston, 1876.
[2] Emended to Pitcheir (Schinz, 1845), Pithechir (Jentink, 1892), Pithechirus (Agassiz, 1842), and Pithecochirus (Gloger, 1841).

Pseudoconomys Rhoads, 1896. Mus (Pseudoconomys) proconodon.
Pseudomys Gray, 1832........ Pseudomys australis.
Rattus Zimmermann, 1777.... Rattus somnolentus, R. migrans.
† **Saccostomus** Peters, 1846..... Saccostomus campestris.
Spalacomys Peters, 1861...... Spalacomys indicus.
? **Tenomys** Rafinesque, 1815.... Nomen nudum.
Trilophomys Depéret, 1892...... New name for *Lophiomys* Depéret, 1890.
Uromys Peters, 1867.......... Mus macropus.
Vandeleuria Gray, 1842....... Mus oleraceus.

NEOTOMINÆ.

Neotominæ MERRIAM, Proc. Acad. Nat. Sci. Phila., pp. 228, Sept. 24, 1894.

Name, authority, and date.	Type or included species.
? *Bothriomys* Ameghino, 1889.....	*Bothriomys catenatus.*
Hodomys Merriam, 1894......	Neotoma alleni.
Nelsonia Merriam, 1897	(See page 277.)
Neotoma Say & Ord, 1825.....	Mus floridanus.
? *Paciculus* Cope, 1879..........	*Paciculus insolitus.*
Plyssophorus Ameghino, 1889...	*Plyssophorus elegans.*
Teonoma Gray, 1843..........	Neotoma drummondii (Myoxus drummondii).
Tretomys Ameghino, 1889.......	*Tretomys atavus.*
Xenomys Merriam, 1892......	Xenomys nelsoni.

OTOMYINÆ.

Otomyinæ THOMAS, Proc. Zool. Soc. London, 1896, p. 1017 (1897).

Name, authority, and date.	Type or included species.
? **Euryotis** Brants, 1827.........	Mus irroratus.
Oreinomys Trouessart, 1881...	New name for Oreomys Heuglin, 1877.
† **Oreomys** Heuglin, 1877........	Oreomys typus.
Otomys F. Cuvier, 1823........	Two species, afterwards named Otomys unisulcatus (Sept., 1829), and O. bisulcatus (Oct., 1829).

PHLŒOMYINÆ.

Phlœomyinæ ALSTON, Proc. Zool. Soc. London, 1876, p. 81.
  Phlœomys Waterhouse, 1839.. Phlœomys cuningi.

RHYNCHOMYINÆ.

Rhynchomyinæ THOMAS, Proc. Zool. Soc. London, 1896, p. 1017 (1897).
  Rhynchomys Thomas, 1895... Rhynchomys soricoides.

SIPHNEINÆ.

Siphneinæ GILL, Arrangement Fam. Mammals, Nov., 1872, p. 20.

262   *Palmer—Generic and Family Names of Rodents.*

Name, authority, and date.	Type or included species.
Myospalax Blyth, 1846	Georychus fuscocapillus.
Myotalpa Kerr, 1792	Mus talpinus, M. capensis, M. maritimus, M. aspalax, Myotalpa typhla.
Siphneus Brants, 1827	Mus aspalax.

OCHOTONIDAE.

‡ **Lagidæ** Schulze, Helios, XIV, p. 82, 1897.
‡ **Lagomina** Gray, Thomson's Ann. Philos., XXVI, p. 341, Nov., 1825.
‡ **Lagomyidæ** Lilljeborg, Syst. Öfvers. Gnag. Däggdjuren, pp. 9, 58, 1866.
Ochotonidæ Thomas, Proc. Zool. Soc. London, 1896, p. 1026 (1897).

Name, authority, and date.	Type or included species.
Abra Gray, 1863.	Lagomys curzoniæ.
* *Amphilagus* Pomel, 1854	*Amphilagus antiquus.*
* *Lagodus* Pomel, 1854	*Lagodus picoides.*
† **Lagomys** G. Cuvier, 1800	Le pika (Lepus alpinus).
Lagopsis Schlosser, 1884	*Lagomys oeningensis, L. verus.*
.* *Marunsiomys*[1] Croizet, 1853	(?)
Myolagus Hensel, 1856	*Lagomys sardus.*
Ochotona Link, 1795	Lepus pusillus, L. alpinus, L. ochotona.
* **Pika** Lacépède, 1799	Lepus alpinus.
* *Platyodon* Bravard, 1853	Nomen nudum.
* *Prolagus* Pomel, 1854	*Lagomys sansaniensis.*
Titanomys Meyer, 1843	*Titanomys visenoviensis.*

OCTODONTIDÆ.[2]

‡ **Aulacodina** Bonaparte, Conspectus Syst. Mastozoologiæ, 1850.
Capromyna Gervais, D'Orbigny's Dict. Univ. d'Hist. Nat., XI, p. 204, 1849.

---

[1] Emended (?) to *Marcuinomys* (Croizet, 1859).
[2] Considerable diversity of opinion exists as to the subdivisions of the Octodonts. Some authors arrange the genera in 3, and others in 4 groups.
Capromyinæ: *Adelphomys*, Aulacodus, Capromys, *Discolomys*, *Eumysops*, *Graphimys*, Guillinomys, *Gyrignophus*, Isodon, *Lomomys*, Mastonotus, *Morenia*, Myocastor, Myopotamus, Mysateles, *Neorcomys*, *Olenopsis*, Ondatra, *Orthomys*, *Paranomys*, Plagiodontia, Potamys, *Pseudoneoreomys*, *Scleromys*, Spaniomys, Stichomys, Triaulacodus, *Tribodon* (?), and Thryonomys.
Ctenodactylinæ: Ctenodactylus, Massoutiera, Pectinator, *Pellegrina*, Petromus, and *Ruscinomys* (?).
Echimyinæ: Carterodon, Cercomys, Dactylomys, Echimys, Isothrix, Kannabateomys, Lasiomys, Lasiuromys, Loncheres, Lonchophorus, Mesomys, Nelomys Jourdan, Nelomys Lund, Phyllomys, Platythrix, Pœcilomys, Thrichomys, and Thrinacodus.
Octodontinæ: Abrocoma, Aconaemys, *Actenomys*, Ctenomys, Dendrobius, *Dicælophorus*, *Dicolpomys*, Octodon, *Phloramys*, *Pithanotomys*, *Platæomys*, Pœphagomys, Psammoryctes, Schizodon, and Spalacopus.

Capromysideæ Lesson, Nouv. Tabl. Règne Animal, Mamm., p. 124, 1842.
Capromyidæ Burmeister, Syst. Uebersicht Thiere Brasil., I, pp. 187, 189, 1854.
Ctenodactylina Gervais, Ann. Sci. Nat., 3ᵐᵒ ser., XX, p. 245, 1853.
Ctenodactylinæ Gill, Arrangement Fam. Mamm., p. 22, Nov., 1872.
Ctenodactylidæ Zittel, Handb. der Palæont., IV, 2ᵗᵉ Lief., p. 542, 1893.
Ctenomysideæ Lesson, Nouv Tabl. Règne Animal, Mamm., p. 105, 1842.
Echymyna Gray, Thomson's Ann. Philos., XXVI, p. 341, Nov., 1825.
Echymyidæ Bonaparte, Conspectus Syst. Mastozoologiæ, 1850.
Echinomyidæ Ameghino, Mam. Fos. Repub. Argentina, in Actas Acad. Nac. Ciencias, Cordoba, VI, p. 131, 1889.
Loncheridæ Burmeister, Syst.Uebers. Thiere Brasil., I, pp. 188,192,1854.
‡ **Muriformidæ** Ameghino, Enum. Sist. Especies Mam. Fós. Patagonia, p. 10, Dic., 1887.
Myiopotamina Bonaparte, Conspectus Syst. Mastozoologiæ, 1850.
Octodontidæ Waterhouse, Proc. Zool. Soc. London, 1839, p. 172.
‡ **Psammoryctina** Wagner, Wiegmann's Archiv f. Naturgesch., 1841, I.
‡ **Psammoryctidæ** Burmeister, Syst. Uebersicht Thiere Brasil., I, pp. 188, 212, 1854.
Spalacopodidæ Lilljeborg, Syst. Öfversigt Gnag. Däggdjuren, pp. 9, 44, 1866. (Spalacopodoïdes Brandt, 1855.)

Name, authority, and date.	Type or included species.
Abrocoma Waterhouse, 1837..	Abrocoma bennettii, A. cuvieri.
Aconaemys Ameghino, 1891...	New name for Schizodon Waterhouse.
Actenomys Burmeister, 1888.....	*Actenomys cuniculinus.*
Adelphomys Ameghino, 1887....	*Adelphomys candidus.*
‡ **Aulacodus** Temminck, 1827...	Aulacodus swinderianus. (See Thryonomys, Triaulacodus.)
Cannabateomys Lydekker, 1892.	Emended form for Kannabateomys.
Capromys Desmarest, 1822.....	Capromys fournieri.
Carterodon Waterhouse, 1848..	Echimys sulcidens.
Cercomys Cuvier, 1829........	Cercomys cunicularius.
Ctenodactylus Gray, 1830.....	Ctenodactylus massonii.
Ctenomys Blainville, 1826.....	Ctenomys brasiliensis.
Dactylomys I. Geoffroy, 1838..	Dactylomys typus.
Dendrobius Meyen, 1833......	Dendrobius degus.
Dicœlophorus Ameghino, 1888...	*Dicœlophorus latidens, D. simplex, D celsus, Ctenomys priscus.*
Dicolpomys Winge, 1887........	*Dicolpomys fossor.*
Discolomys Ameghino, 1889.....	*Discolomys cuneus.*
Echimys[1] Cuvier, 1809........	Echimys cristatus, E. spinosus.
Eumysops Ameghino, 1888	*Eumysops plicatus, E. læviplicatus, E. robustus.*
Graphimys Ameghino, 1891.....	*Graphimys provectus.*
Guillinomys Lesson, 1842.....	Guillinomys chilensis.

---

[1] Emended to Echinomys (Wagner, 1840), Enchomys (Gloger, 1841).

Gundi (' Fischer ') Lataste, 1881 A common name for Ctenodactylus,
          erroneously credited to Fischer as
          a genus.

Gyrignophus Ameghino, 1891 ... *Gyrignophus complicatus.*

Habrocoma Wagner, 1842..... Emended form for Abrocoma.

Houtia Agassiz, 1842....... .. Nomen nudum. Native name for
          Capromys, included by Agassiz in
          list of genera, without reference or
          mention of species.

† **Isodon** Say, 1822.............. Isodon pilorides.

Isothrix Wagner, 1845........ Isothrix bistriata, I. pachyura, I. pa-
          gurus.

Kannabateomys Jentink, 1891 Dactylomys amblyonyx.

Lasiomys Burmeister, 1854.... Lasiomys hirsutus.

Lasiuromys Deville, 1852...... Lasiuromys villosus.

Lomomys Ameghino, 1891 ..... *Lomomys evexus.*

Loncheres[1] Illiger, 1811...... Loncheres paleacea, Hystrix chrysuros.

Lonchophorus Lund, 1839...:... *Lonchophorus fossilis.*

Massoutiera Lataste, 1885..... Ctenodactylus mzabi.

Mastonotus Wesmael, 1841.... Mastonotus popelairi (= Mus coypus.)

Mesomys Wagner, 1845....... Mesomys ecaudatus.

Morenia Ameghino, 1886........ *Morenia elephantina.*

Myocastor Kerr, 1792........ Mus (Myocastor) coypus (type), Mus
          (M.) zibethicus.

Myopotamus Geoffroy, 1805... Myopotamus bonariensis.

Mysateles Lesson, 1842 .... Mysateles poeppingii (= Capromys
          prehensilis).

Nelomys Jourdan, 1837....... Echimys cristatus.

† **Nelomys** Lund, 1841.......... Echimys antricola, E. sulcidens. (See
          Thrichomys.)

Neoreomys Ameghino, 1887..... *Neoreomys australis, N. indivisus, N.*
          decisus.

Octodon Bennett, 1832........ Octodon cumingii.

Olenopsis Ameghino, 1889....... *Olenopsis uncinus.*

* **Ondatra** Link, 1795........... Mus coypus, Castor zibethicus.

Orthomys Ameghino, 1881...... *Orthomys dentatus.*

Orycteromys('Blainville')Agas- Used by Blainville in 1826, only in
  siz, 1842.   the French form Orctérome, for the
          genus described as Ctenomys. (See
          Orycteromys, p. 256.)

Paranomys (Scalabrini MS.) Ame-
  ghino, 1889. .... *Paranomys typicus.*

Pectinator Blyth, 1856........ Pectinator spekei.

Pellegrina Gregorio, 1886....... *Pellegrina panormensis.*

Petromus A. Smith, 1831...... Petromus typicus.

Phloramys Ameghino, 1887.. ... *Phloramys homogenidens.*

---

[1] Emended to Loncherites (London Encyclopœdia, 1845).

Phyllomys Lund, 1839........ Phyllomys brasiliensis (?)
Pithanotomys Ameghino, 1887... *Pithanotomys columnaris.*
Plagiodontia[1] F. Cuvier, 1836. Plagiodontia aedium.
* *Platacomys* Ameghino, 1881..... *Platacomys scindens.*
* **Platythrix** Pictet, 1842........ (?)
* **Pœcilomys** Pictet, 1842....... (?)
Pœphagomys F. Cuvier, 1834.. Pœphagomys ater.
Potamys Larranhaga, 1823. Le quyia of Azara (Myopotamus coypus).
Psammoryctes Pœppig, 1835.. Psammoryctes noctivagus (= Spalacopus pœppigii).
Pseudoneoreomys Ameghino, 1891 *Pseudoneoreomys pachyrhynchus, P. leptorhynchus, P. mesorhynchus.*
? *Ruscinomys* Depéret, 1890...... *Ruscinomys europæus.*
† **Schizodon** Waterhouse, 1842.. Schizodon fuscus. (See Aconaemys.)
Scleromys Ameghino, 1887...... *Scleromys angustus.*
Spalacopus Wagler, 1832 .... Spalacopus pœppigii.
Spaniomys Ameghino, 1887..... *Spaniomys riparius, S. modestus.*
Stichomys Ameghino, 1887...... *Stichomys regularis, S. constans.*
Thrichomys Trouessart, 1881.. Thrichomys antricola, T. inermis, T. brevicauda.
Thrinacodus Günther, 1879... Thrinacodus albicauda.
Thryonomys Fitzinger, 1867... Aulacodus semipalmatus.
Triaulacodus Lydekker, 1896.. New name for Aulacodus Temminck, 1827. (See Thryonomys.)
Tribodon Ameghino, 1887...... *Tribodon clemens.*

PEDETIDÆ.

‡ **Halamydæ** Gray, London Medical Repository, XV, p. 303, April 1, 1821.
Pedestina Gray, Thomson's Ann. Philos., XXVI, p. 342, Nov., 1825.
Pedetidæ Gill, Arrangement Fam. Mamm., p. 20, Nov., 1872.

Name, authority, and date.	Type or included species.
Helamys F. Cuvier, 1817......	Mus cafer.
Lagotis Blainville, 1817.......	'La grande gerboise du Cap.'
Pedetes Illiger, 1811..........	Dipus cafer.

PSEUDOSCIURIDÆ.

Pseudosciuridæ Zittel, Handb. der Palæont., IV, 2te Lief., p. 523, 1893.

Name, authority, and date.	Type or included species.
Adelomys Gervais, 1853......	*Theridomys vaillanti.* (See *Theridomyidæ.*)
? *Decticadapis* Lemoine, 1883.....	*Decticadapis sciuroides.*
Pseudosciurus Hensel, 1856......	*Pseudosciurus succicus.*
Sciurodon Schlosser, 1884.......	*Sciurodon cadurcense.*
Sciuroides Forsyth Major, 1873..	*Sciurus rutimeyeri, Sciuroides fraasi, S. siderolithicus, S. minimus.*

---

[1] Emended to Plagiodon (Alston, 1876).

SCIURIDÆ.

Allomyidæ MARSH, Am. Journ. Sci., 3d ser., XIV, p. 253, Sept., 1877.
Arctomydæ GRAY, London Med. Repository, XV, p. 303, April 1, 1821.
Arctomysideæ LESSON, Nouv. Tabl. Règne Animal, Mamm.,p.115,1842.
‡ **Campsiurina** BRANDT, fide CARUS, Handb. Zool., p. 96, 1868–'75.
Leithiidæ LYDEKKER, Proc. Zool. Soc. London, 1895, p. 862 (1896).
Nannosciurinæ FORSYTH MAJOR, Proc. Zool. Soc. London, 1893, pp. 187, 189.
Pteromidæ ANDERSON, Yunnan Exped., p. 278, 1879.
Sciuridæ GRAY, London Medical Repository, XV, p. 304, April 1, 1821.

Name, authority, and date.	Type or included species.
Allomys Marsh, 1877	*Allomys nitens.*
Ammospermophilus Merriam, 1892.	Tamias leucurus.
Amphisciurus (Bravard MS.) Lydekker, 1885	*Amphisciurus typus.*
Anisonyx Rafinesque, 1817	Anisonyx brachiura (= Arctomys columbianus).
Arctomys Schreber, 1780	Arctomys marmota, A. monax, A. bobac, A. empetra, A. citillus.
Atlantoxerus Forsyth Major, 1893.	Xerus getulus.
Baginia Gray, 1867	Sciurus platani.
Callosciurus Gray, 1867	Sciurus rafflesii.
Callospermophilus Merriam, 1897.	Sciurus lateralis.
Citillus Lichtenstein, 1827–'34.	Citillus mexicanus, C. leptodactylus, C. mugosaricus.
Colobotis Brandt, 1844	Spermophilus fulvus.
Cynomys Rafinesque, 1817	Cynomys socialis, C. grisea.
Echinosciurus Trouessart,1880.	Sciurus hypopyrrhus (type), S. variabilis, S. stramineus.
Eosciurus Trouessart, 1880	Sciurus bicolor (type), S. giganteus, S. indicus, S. maximus, S. macrurus.
Eoxerus Forsyth Major, 1893.	Xerus laticaudatus, X. berdmorei, X. tristriatus, X. palmarum, X. insignis, X. hosei.
Erythrosciurus Gray, 1867	Sciurus ferrugineus, S. siamensis.
Eupetaurus Thomas, 1888	Eupetaurus cinereus.
Eutamias Trouessart, 1880	Tamias asiaticus (type), T. harrisi, T. lateralis, *T. laevidens.*
Farunculus('Lesson')Gray,1867.	Probably a misprint for Funambulus.
Funambulus Lesson, 1832	Funambulus indicus.
Funisciurus Trouessart, 1880	Sciurus lemniscatus.
Geosciurus A. Smith, 1834	Sciurus erythopus.
Guerlinguetus Gray, 1821	Sciurus guerlinguetus.
Heliosciurus Trouessart, 1880	Sciurus annulatus.
Heterosciurus Trouessart,1880.	Sciurus ferrugineus.

Ictidomys J. A. Allen, 1877... Spermophilus tereticaudus, S. mexicanus, S. 13-lineatus (type), S. franklini.

Lagomys Storr, 1780.......... "An unnatural and undefined combination of forms with squat bodies [including 24 species], but typified by species of Arctomys."—Gill.

† **Laria** Gray, 1867... .... Sciurus insignis.

Leithia[1] Lydekker, 1896........ *Myoxus melitensis.*

Lipura Illiger, 1811............ Hyrax hudsonius.

Macroxus Cuvier, 1823........ Le guerlinguet et le toupaye.

* **Marmota** Blumenbach, 1779... Marmota alpina, M. cricetus, M. lemmus, M. typhlus, M. capensis.[2]

Meniscomys Cope, 1878.......... *Meniscomys hippodus, M. multiplicatus.*

Microsciurus J. À. Allen, 1895. Sciurus (Microsciurus) alfari.

Monax Warden, 1819......... Monax missouriensis (= Cynomys ludovicianus).

Nannosciurus Trouessart, 1880. Sciurus melanotis, S. exilis.

Neosciurus Trouessart, 1880... Sciurus carolinensis (type), S. arizonensis, S. griseoflavus, S. aberti, S. fossor.

Otocolobus Brandt, 1844...... Synonym of Colobotis (?).

Otospermophilus Brandt, 1844. Spermophilus beecheyi.

Palæosciurus Pomel, 1854....... *Sciurus (Palæosciurus) feignouxii, S. (P.) chalaniati.*

Palmista Gray, 1867.......... Sciurus palmarum, S. penicillatus, S. layardii, S. sublineatus.

Parasciurus Trouessart, 1880... Sciurus niger.

Paraxerus Forsyth Major, 1893. Xerus cepapi, X. palliatus, X. pyrropus, X. congicus, X. lemniscatus, X. isabella, X. boehmi.

Petaurista Link, 1795......... Sciurus volucella, S. volans, S. hudsonius, S. petaurista (type), S. sagitta.

Plesiarctomys Bravard, 1848-'52. *Plesiarctomys gervaisii.*

Plesispermophilus Filhol, 1883... *Plesispermophilus angustidens.*

Protoxerus Forsyth Major, 1893. Sciurus stangeri, S. ebii, S. aubinnii.

Pteromys G. Cuvier, 1800..... Sciurus volans, S. petaurista.

Pterotix Rafinesque, 1815.. .. Nomen nudum.

Ratufa Gray, 1867............ Sciurus indicus.

Rheithrosciurus[3] Gray, 1867.. Sciurus macrotis.

Rhinosciurus Gray, 1843 ..... Rhinosciurus tupaioides.

---

[1] This genus is only provisionally referred to the Sciuridæ. Lydekker has recently suggested a special family, *Leithiidæ*, for it.

[2] From the 7th edition of the Handbuch d. Naturgeschichte, 1803. The first edition, 1779, not seen.

[3] Emended to Rhithrosciurus (Lydekker, 1891).

Rukaia Gray, 1867............ Sciurus macrourus, S. bicolor, S. ephippium.
Sciuropterus F. Cuvier, 1825.. Sciurus volans.
Sciurus Linnæus, 1758........ Sciurus vulgaris, S. niger, S. cinereus, S. flavus, S. getulus, S. striatus, S. volans.
Spermophilopsis Blasius, 1884. Spermophilus leptodactylus.
Spermophilus F. Cuvier, 1825. Mus citillus.
Spermosciurus Lesson, 1836... Includes 12 species, mostly from Africa.
Stereodectes Cope, 1869 .... *Stereodectes tortus.*
Tamias Illiger, 1811........... Sciurus striatus.
Tamiasciurus Trouessart, 1880. Sciurus hudsonicus.
Tenotis Rafinesque, 1817...... Tenotis griseus (= Sciurus erithopus).
Xerospermophilus Merriam, 1892. Spermophilus mohavensis.
* **Xerus** Hemprich & Ehrenberg, 1832. Xerus brachyotus (and X. syriacus?).

SPALACIDÆ.[1]

‡ **Aspalacidæ** GRAY, Thomson's Ann. Philos., XXVI, p. 342, Nov., 1825.
Aspalomyina WATERHOUSE, Ann. & Mag. Nat. Hist., X, p. 203, 1842.
Rhizomyinæ THOMAS, Proc. Zool. Soc. London, 1896, p. 1021 (1897).
Spalacidæ GRAY, London Med. Repository, XV, p. 303, April 1, 1821.

Name, authority, and date.	Type or included species.
Aspalax Desmarest, 1804......	Mus typhlus.
* **Aspalomys** Laxmann........	(?)
Chrysomys Gray, 1843........	Bathyergus splendens.
Nyctocleptes Temminck, 1832.	Nyctocleptes dekan (= Mus sumatrensis).
Ommatostergus Nordmann, 1840.	Ommatostergus pallasii.
Rhizomys Gray, 1831.........	Rhizomys sinensis, R. sumatrensis.
Spalax Güldenstädt, 1770.....	Spalax microphthalmus (= S. typhlus Pall., 1778).
Tachyoryctes Rüppell, 1835...	Bathyergus splendens.
* **Talpoides** Lacépède, 1799......	Mus typhlus.
Typhlodon Falconer, 1868.......	Nomen nudum (*Rhizomys sivalensis* Lydekker, 1878?)

THERIDOMYIDÆ.

Theridomyidæ ALSTON, Proc. Zool. Soc. London, 1876, pp. 70, 88.
Trechomyinæ TROUESSART, Cat. Mamm. tam viv. quam foss, p. 392, 1897.

---

[1] Chrysomys, Nyctocleptes, Rhizomys, Tachyoryctes and *Typhlodon* belong to the Rhizomyinæ; Aspalax, Aspalomys, Ommatostergus, Talpoides, and Spalax to the Spalacinæ.

Name, authority, and date.	Type or included species.
Adelomys Gervais, 1853......	*Theridomys raillanti.* (See *Pseudosciuridæ.*)
Archæomys Laizer & Parieu, 1839.	New name for *Palæomys* Laiz. & Par.
Blainvillimys (Bravard MS.) Gervais, 1848-'52	*Theridomys blainvillei.*
Cournomys (Croizet) Zittel, 1893.	Synonym of *Issidioromys.*
Cuvierimys Bravard, 1848-'52....	*Cuvierimys laurillardi.*
Dipoides Jäger, 1835.....	Species not named.
Gergoviomys (Croizet MS.) Blainville, 1840...	Species not named.
* *Isoptychus* Pomel, 1854....... ..	*Theridomys* (*Isoptychus*) *jourdani, Isoptychus auberyi, I. antiquus, I. cuvieri, I. rassoni, Theridomys aquatilis* (?).
Issidioromys (Croizet MS.) Blainville, 1840............... ...	*Issidioromys pseudanæma* Gervais, 1848.
† *Neomys* Bravard, 1844..........	*Neomys lembronicus* (= *Theridomys lembronicus*).
Nesokerodon Schlosser, 1884.....	*Isiodoromys minor.*
* *Omegodus* Pomel, 1854..........	*Omegodus echimyoides.*
* *Palanæma* Pomel, 1854........	*Palanæma antiquus.*
† *Palæomys* Laizer & Parieu, 1839..	*Palæomys arvernensis.* (See *Archæomys.*)
* *Perrieromys* Croizet.............	(?)
Protechimys Schlosser, 1884.....	*Protechimys gracilis, P. major.*
*†*Tæniodus* Pomel, 1854..........	*Echimys curvistriatus.*
Theridomys Jourdan, 1837.......	Species not named in first description.
Trechomys Lartet, 1869........	*Trechomys bonduellii.*

INCERTÆ SEDIS.

Anotis Rafinesque, 1815.......	Nomen nudum.
Archilagus Haeckel, 1895.......	Hypothetical genus —'Atavus omnium Rodentium.'
Asteromys[1] Ameghino, 1897.....	*Asteromys punctus, A. prospicuus.*
Budomys('Croizet') Bravard,1843	Nomen nudum.
Cephalomys[1] Ameghino, 1897....	*Cephalomys arcidens, C. plexus.*
Haplostropha Ameghino, 1891...	*Haplostropha scalabriniana.*
Hystriocomys Giebel, 1860.......	*Hystriocomys thuringiacus.*
? *Mixodectes*[2] Cope, 1883....... ..	*Mixodectes pungens, M. crassiculus.*
Orchiomys[1] Ameghino, 1897.....	*Orchiomys prostans.*

[1] *Cephalomyidæ* Ameghino, Bol. Inst. Geog. Argentino, XVIII, p. 592, Oct. 6, 1897.

[2] *Mixodectidæ* Cope, Proc. Acad. Nat. Sci. Phila., p. 80, May 22, 1883.

"The discovery of some skeleton fragments in good association with a lower jaw of *Mixodectus pungens* makes it probable that this genus should be removed from the Primates and placed as an extremely primitive Rodent."—Matthew, Bull. Am. Mus. Nat. Hist. New York, IX, p. 265, 1897.

Palaiotrogus Jäger, 1839..... ... *Palaiotrogus steinheimensis.*
Paradoxomys[1] Ameghino, 1885.. *Paradoxomys cancricorus.*
Protechynus Filhol, 1891........ Nomen nudum.
Protoptychus[2] Scott, 1895........ *Protoptychus hatcheri.*

[1] *Paradoxomyina* Ameghino, Bol. Acad. Nac.Cien.,Córdoba, IX, p. 79, 1886.
Paradoxomydæ Ameghino, Mam. Fos. Repub. Argentina, in Actas Acad. Nac. Ciencias, Córdoba, VI, p. 122, 1889.

[2] "The genus is probably to be regarded as the ancestral type of the Dipodidæ, and indicates an American origin for this family."—Scott, Proc. Acad. Nat. Sci. Phila., 1895, p. 286.

INDEX OF GENERIC NAMES.